Rabbit and Big Cat

Retold by Teresa Heapy
Illustrated by Mia Powell

OXFORD
UNIVERSITY PRESS

Big Cat licks and licks.

Rabbit runs up to the top.

Rabbit pulls.

Then he licks and licks.

Rabbit has a shock.

Rabbit thinks.

I can rub it on.

Big Cat runs up to the top.

Rabbit hops off.
Big Cat is sad.

Rabbit runs off.

No, Rabbit!

Retell the story

Once upon a time ...

The end

The Mitten

Retold by Sarah Snashall
Illustrated by Katie Rewse

OXFORD
UNIVERSITY PRESS

The mitten is not in the pocket.

Cat pats the thing.

Cat gets in.

Kitten gets in.

Push up, Cat.

Hen gets in.

Chick gets in.

Push up, Chick.

Moth gets in.

It is a big shock.

The mitten is in bits!

A bed in the shed!

Retell the story

Once upon a time …

The end

Sinbad

Retold by Jane Langford
Illustrated by Wazza Pink

OXFORD
UNIVERSITY PRESS

He has things to sell.

The ship is in thick fog.

The ship hits a big rock.

bang!

It is not a rock.

It is a big fish!

The fish sinks and Sinbad gets on a log.

He kicks and pushes.

A man pulls Sinbad back on to a ship.

Thanks.

Sinbad is in luck. It is his ship.

His box is on the deck.

Sinbad sells his things.

Sinbad gets back on the ship.

Yes! I am rich.

He has lots to tell.

I sat on a big fish!

Retell the story

Once upon a time ...

The end

The Ram

Retold by Paul Shipton
Illustrated by Tamara Anegon

OXFORD
UNIVERSITY PRESS

The ram fed on the bush.

"Go, ram!"

The ram did not go.

I will tell the ram to go.

Go, ram!

The ram ran at the cat.

I will tell the ram to go.

Go, ram!

The ram sat on the chicken.

I will tell the ram to go.

Go, ram!

"No!"

The ram hit the dog.

I can tell the ram to go.

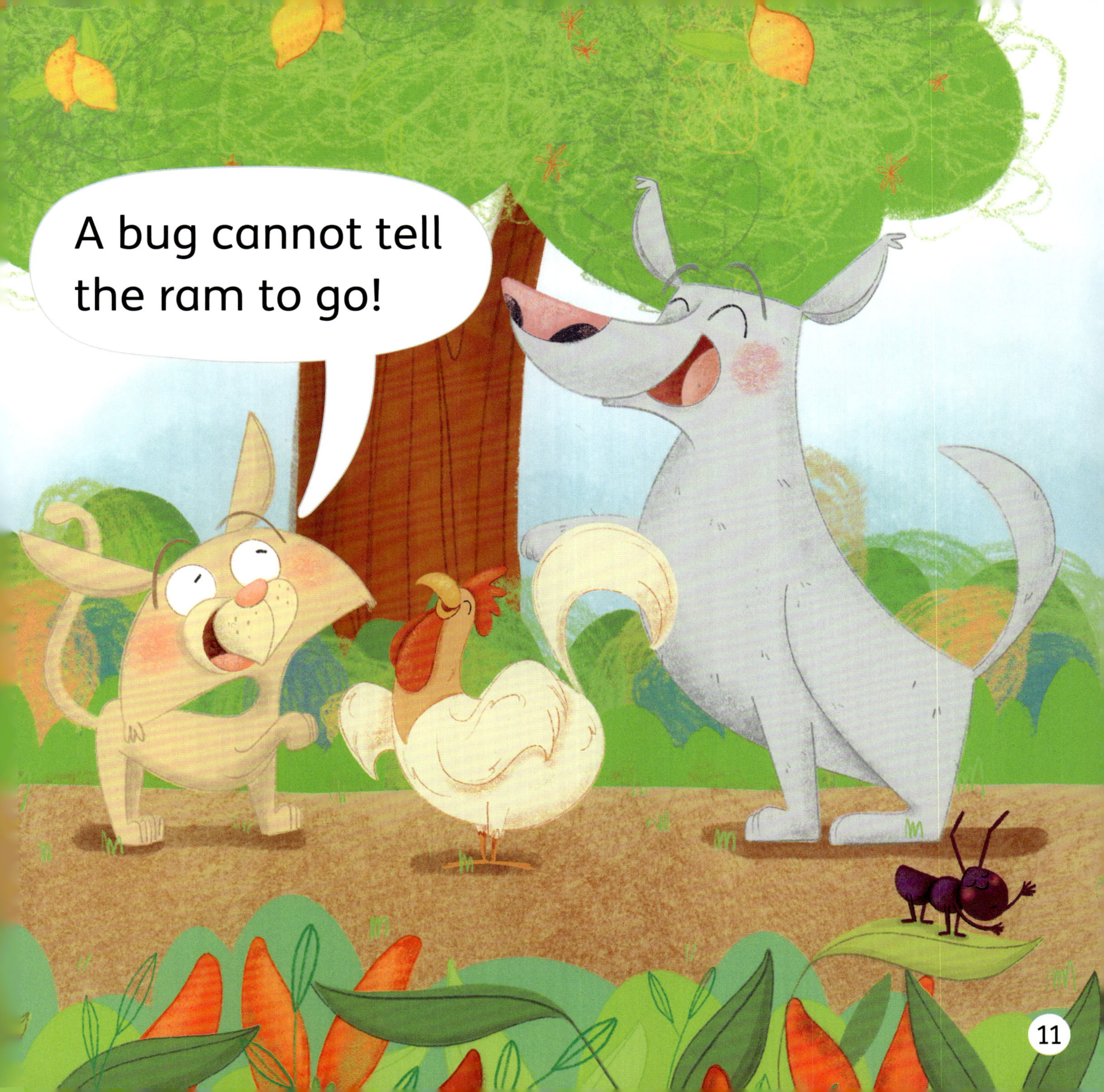
A bug cannot tell
the ram to go!

The bug ran up to the ram.

He ran up a back leg.

Then the bug bit the ram.

The ram ran off.

Retell the story

Once upon a time ...

The end